WORKBOOK FOR

EMOTIONAL

INTELLIGENCE HABITS

A TRANSFORMATIVE GUIDE

THROUGH THE INTRICATE

LANDSCAPE OF EMOTIONAL

INTELLIGENCE

BY

ARABELLA SCOTT

1

INTRODUCTION:

Welcome to the transformative journey of "Emotional Intelligence Habits" — a comprehensive workbook designed to guide you through the intricate landscape of emotional intelligence over the course of four enriching weeks. Within these pages, you'll find a roadmap to cultivate emotional intelligence through practical strategies, fostering self-awareness, self-management, social awareness, and relationship management.

Emotional intelligence, often referred to as EQ, is the vital skill that shapes our interactions, influences our decision-making, and ultimately impacts our success and well-being. Backed by the expertise of Dr. Travis Bradberry, renowned for translating complex concepts into actionable behaviors, this workbook is a culmination of decades of research in psychology and neuroscience, distilled into accessible steps that can be seamlessly integrated into your daily life.

In these pages, you'll discover a profound truth: while EQ may be inherent, it can also be developed, nurtured, and honed. The journey begins with the foundation of self-awareness – the cornerstone of emotional intelligence. By recognizing and understanding your emotions, triggers, and responses, you'll set the stage for a deep exploration of the emotional landscape.

From there, you'll delve into mastering self-management techniques that empower you to regulate your emotions, manage stress, and bolster self-control. These skills will serve as tools for creating a harmonious internal environment, enabling you to navigate challenges with poise and resilience.

As the journey unfolds, you'll nurture your social awareness and empathy, unlocking the power of connection. You'll learn to read nonverbal cues, practice empathetic listening, and build stronger relationships through active engagement. By developing these skills, you'll create a web of authentic interactions that uplift both you and those around you.

Finally, you'll excel in the art of relationship management, an integral aspect of emotional intelligence. You'll acquire conflict resolution techniques, establish clear communication channels, recognize toxic influences, and even learn how to become a supportive and influential leader in various domains of your life.

As you embark on this journey, remember that change is gradual, and transformation is a process. Each week's activities are not merely tasks; they are building blocks that contribute to the grand tapestry of emotional intelligence. Embrace each step, each exercise, and each reflection as an opportunity to uncover new layers of self-awareness, empathy, and growth.

Are you ready to embark on a path that leads to greater self-mastery, improved relationships, and a more fulfilling life? The journey starts now. Let's delve into the rich content of "Emotional Intelligence Habits," and may these pages become your guide to unlocking the potential within you.

WEEK 1

BUILDING THE FOUNDATION OF

SELF-AWARENESS

Welcome to Week 1 of your journey towards enhancing your emotional intelligence through the power of self-awareness. This week is all about laying the groundwork for a deeper understanding of yourself, your emotions, and how they influence your actions. As you delve into the activities and insights of this week, you'll embark on a transformative process that will unlock the doors to personal growth, improved relationships, and greater overall well-being.

Imagine gaining the ability to navigate through life's challenges with an increased sense of clarity and purpose. Envision having a heightened awareness of your emotions and triggers, enabling you to respond thoughtfully rather than react impulsively. As you immerse yourself in the contents of this week, you'll soon realize that self-awareness is not just a buzzword; it's a fundamental skill that can profoundly impact your life.

Understanding the Importance of Self-Awareness

Self-awareness is the cornerstone of emotional intelligence, and it serves as the launchpad for your personal growth journey. This week, we'll dive deep into why self-awareness matters and how it can positively influence every aspect of your life. By recognizing the link between self-awareness and emotional intelligence, you'll gain a clear understanding of why investing in this skill is worth every effort.

Recognizing Your Emotional Triggers

Have you ever found yourself reacting strongly to certain situations or people without

13

quite understanding why? In this section, we'll explore the concept of emotional triggers – those underlying factors that spark emotional responses within you. By identifying these triggers, you'll begin to unravel the complex web of emotions that influence your behavior. This newfound awareness will empower you to manage your reactions more effectively and with greater intention.

Practicing Mindfulness for Increased Self-Awareness

Mindfulness is a powerful tool that can help you tune into your thoughts, feelings, and bodily sensations. This week, you'll engage in mindfulness exercises designed to enhance your self-awareness. Through these practices, you'll learn to observe your emotions without judgment, cultivating a deeper understanding of your internal landscape. Mindfulness will enable you to detach from automatic reactions and respond to situations in ways that align with your true values.

Cultivating Emotional Self-Awareness through Reflection

Self-reflection is the key to unlocking the door to your emotions and thought patterns. By dedicating time to introspection, you'll uncover hidden layers of your emotional world. This week, we'll guide you through reflective exercises that encourage you to explore your past experiences, thought processes, and emotional responses. As you delve into your inner self, you'll gain insights that pave the way for enhanced emotional self-awareness.

Leveraging Self-Awareness for Improved Decision-Making

Imagine being able to make decisions with confidence, knowing that your choices align with your values and aspirations. In this section, we'll explore how self-awareness directly influences your decision-making process. By understanding your

17

emotions and motives, you'll become better equipped to make choices that support your long-term goals. Through self-awareness, you'll learn to navigate the intricate balance between logic and emotions, leading to more informed and thoughtful decisions.

As you conclude Week 1, take a moment to reflect on the journey you've begun. You've delved into the importance of self-awareness, discovered your emotional triggers, practiced mindfulness, engaged in self-reflection, and explored the connection between self-awareness and decision-making. This is just the beginning of your transformational path towards enhanced emotional intelligence.

EXERCISES

1. **Mindful Breathing**: Spend 10 minutes each day practicing deep, intentional breathing. Focus on your breath as it enters and leaves your body. Observe any thoughts or

emotions that arise without judgment.

2. **Emotion Journal**: Create a journal to track your emotional responses throughout the week. Note down situations that triggered strong emotions and reflect on why you reacted the way you did.

3. **Mirror Reflection**: Stand in front of a mirror and spend a few minutes observing your facial expressions. Notice any emotions that arise and

consider their underlying causes.

4. **Daily Check-In**: Set aside a few minutes each evening to reflect on your day. Consider the emotions you experienced, their triggers, and how you managed them.

5. **Values Alignment**: Make a list of your core values. Reflect on how your actions and decisions align with these values, and identify areas where there might be discrepancies.

21

QUESTIONS

1. How can a deeper understanding of your emotional triggers benefit your relationships?

2. How might practicing mindfulness enhance your ability to manage stress?

3. What insights did you gain through the reflective exercises this week?

4. In what ways can self-awareness contribute to

making more informed decisions?

5. How do you envision your life changing as you continue to cultivate self-awareness?

ACTION PLANS

1. Schedule regular mindfulness sessions to continue honing your awareness of the present moment.

2. Create a habit of recording your emotional responses in your journal, noting the circumstances and triggers.

3. Dedicate time for weekly self-reflection, exploring your thoughts, feelings, and experiences in depth.

4. Experiment with applying your increased self-awareness to make conscious decisions in your daily life.

5. Share your insights and experiences with a friend or family member, encouraging them to join you on the journey to enhanced self-awareness.

AFFIRMATIONS

1. "I embrace the power of self-awareness to transform my emotional landscape."

2. "Each moment of mindfulness brings me closer to a deeper understanding of myself."

3. "Through reflection, I uncover the wisdom hidden within my emotions."

4. "My decisions are informed by both my rational mind and my emotional intelligence."

5. "I am committed to the journey of self-awareness, knowing it leads to greater self-mastery."

WEEK 2

MASTERING SELF-

MANAGEMENT TECHNIQUES

Welcome to Week 2 of your journey towards enhancing your emotional intelligence through the mastery of self-management techniques. As you embark on this week's activities, you're delving into the art of harnessing your emotions, effectively managing stress, and cultivating self-control. This week holds the promise of providing you with

27

invaluable tools that will enable you to navigate life's challenges with grace, maintain your equilibrium in the face of stressors, and achieve your personal and professional aspirations.

Imagine having the ability to navigate through difficult situations with calmness and composure. Picture yourself maintaining your focus and determination in the midst of chaos, while fostering a sense of balance in your life. As you immerse yourself in the contents of this week, you'll realize that self-management is not just a skill, but a way of life that can lead to lasting well-being.

Embracing Emotional Regulation Strategies

Emotions are an integral part of the human experience, but learning how to regulate them is an essential skill for emotional intelligence. In this section, you'll explore a variety of strategies that can help you identify, understand, and manage your emotions effectively. By embracing emotional regulation techniques, you'll gain the ability to respond to situations with emotional intelligence rather than being controlled by impulsive reactions.

Developing Effective Stress Management Habits

Stress is an inevitable part of life, but how you manage it can significantly impact your overall well-being. This week, you'll delve into the world of stress management and uncover techniques that can help you alleviate the harmful effects of stress. By developing effective stress management habits, you'll not only protect your physical and mental health but also enhance your emotional resilience.

Enhancing Self-Control and Willpower

Self-control and willpower are like muscles that can be strengthened through practice and conscious effort. In this section, you'll learn how to resist immediate gratification, make better choices, and stay committed to your long-term goals. Through exercises and insights, you'll discover how to enhance your self-discipline and exert control over your impulses, leading to more intentional actions and improved emotional intelligence.

Establishing Healthy Daily Routines

The way you structure your daily routines has a profound impact on your emotional well-being. In this section, you'll explore the significance of creating healthy habits that support your emotional and mental health. By establishing routines that prioritize self-care, relaxation, and reflection, you'll be better equipped to manage your emotions and maintain a balanced life.

Applying Self-Management to Achieve Personal and Professional Goals

Self-management is a crucial skill for achieving your aspirations, whether they are personal or professional. In this final section, you'll learn how to apply the self-management techniques you've explored throughout the week to propel yourself towards success. By effectively managing your emotions, stress, and impulses, you'll be better equipped to overcome challenges, stay focused, and make steady progress towards your goals.

As you conclude Week 2, take a moment to reflect on the

progress you've made. You've learned to embrace emotional regulation, develop stress management habits, enhance self-control, establish healthy routines, and apply self-management for goal achievement. These tools are now in your hands, empowering you to navigate the complexities of life with greater emotional intelligence.

EXERCISES

1. **Emotion Check-In**: Set aside moments throughout the day to check in with your emotions. Acknowledge how you're feeling without judgment and identify any triggers.

2. **Stress-Relief Techniques**: Experiment with various stress-relief techniques such as deep breathing, meditation, or physical activity. Discover which ones resonate with you.

3. **Willpower Challenges**: Choose a small area of your life (e.g., diet, technology use) and set a willpower challenge. Track your progress and reflect on your ability to resist impulses.

4. **Daily Reflection**: Dedicate a few minutes each evening to reflect on your day. Consider how you managed your emotions, stress, and self-control, and identify areas for improvement.

5. **Goal-Oriented Planning**: Select a personal or professional goal and break it down into actionable steps. Create a plan that incorporates self-management techniques to support your journey.

QUESTIONS

1. How does emotional regulation contribute to better decision-making in challenging situations?

2. What stress management techniques resonate with you

and how do they impact your overall well-being?

3. In what ways have you observed self-control positively influencing your daily choices?

4. How can establishing healthy daily routines enhance your emotional resilience?

5. What are some examples of personal or professional goals that would benefit from effective self-management techniques?

ACTION PLANS

1. Integrate brief emotion check-ins throughout your day to stay attuned to your emotional state.

2. Create a personalized stress-relief toolkit that includes multiple techniques for managing stress.

3. Set specific willpower challenges to enhance your self-discipline and evaluate your progress regularly.

4. Design a daily routine that prioritizes self-care,

relaxation, and opportunities for self-reflection.

5. Apply self-management techniques to your chosen goal, monitoring your progress and adjusting as needed.

AFFIRMATIONS

1. "I am in control of my emotions, and I respond to challenges with clarity and poise."

2. "I embrace stress-relief techniques that nurture my

well-being and emotional equilibrium."

3. "My willpower grows stronger with every choice I make in alignment with my goals."

4. "My daily routines support my emotional health and foster a sense of balance."

5. "I am a master of self-management, propelling myself towards my aspirations with purpose."

WEEK 3

NURTURING SOCIAL

AWARENESS AND EMPATHY

Welcome to Week 3 of your journey towards enriching your emotional intelligence through the nurturing of social awareness and empathy. As you step into this week's activities, you're embarking on a voyage that will enable you to forge deeper connections, read nonverbal cues more effectively, and communicate with a

43

heightened level of empathy. This week promises to open up a world of understanding, compassion, and improved relationships, both personally and professionally.

Imagine being able to truly grasp the emotions of others, sensing their needs even when unspoken. Picture yourself engaging in conversations with a profound sense of empathy, leading to more meaningful interactions. As you delve into the contents of this week, you'll recognize that social awareness and empathy are not just interpersonal skills; they are gateways to stronger connections and a richer emotional landscape.

Exploring the Significance of Social Awareness

Social awareness is the key to unlocking a deeper understanding of the people around you and the world at large. In this section, you'll delve into why social awareness is a vital component of emotional intelligence. By recognizing the value of tuning into the emotions, perspectives, and needs of others, you'll discover how this skill can enhance your relationships and enrich your life.

Learning to Read Nonverbal Cues and Body Language

Communication is not just about words; it's also about what remains unspoken. In this segment, you'll explore the intricate world of nonverbal cues and body language. By honing your ability to interpret gestures, facial expressions, and other nonverbal signals, you'll uncover hidden layers of meaning in conversations and deepen your understanding of others.

Practicing Empathetic Listening and Understanding Others' Emotions

Empathy is the cornerstone of emotional intelligence, and empathetic listening is a powerful tool that fosters meaningful connections. In this part of the week, you'll discover the art of truly hearing others and validating their emotions. By practicing empathetic listening, you'll create a safe space for others to express themselves, strengthening your relationships and fostering a sense of trust.

Building Stronger Connections through Active Engagement

Meaningful connections require active engagement. In this section, you'll explore how to be fully present in your interactions, whether with friends, family, colleagues, or acquaintances. By engaging actively, you'll demonstrate genuine interest, ask meaningful questions, and create an environment where authentic conversations can flourish.

Applying Social Awareness to Enhance Communication and Relationships

The culmination of this week's journey lies in applying your newfound social awareness and empathy skills to your interactions. In this final section, you'll learn how to use your enhanced understanding of others to navigate conflicts, communicate effectively, and strengthen your relationships. By applying social awareness, you'll be better equipped to create positive and lasting impacts on those around you.

As you conclude Week 3, take a moment to reflect on the insights you've gained. You've explored the significance of social awareness, learned to read nonverbal cues, practiced empathetic listening, built stronger connections, and discovered how to apply social awareness for enhanced communication and relationships. These skills are now at your fingertips, empowering you to create more profound connections and enrich your emotional intelligence journey.

EXERCISES

1. **Nonverbal Observation:** Engage in a social setting and focus on observing nonverbal

cues and body language. Reflect on the emotions and intentions they convey.

2. **Empathetic Reflection**: After a conversation, take a moment to reflect on the emotions the other person might have felt. Consider their perspective and emotions.

3. **Active Listening Practice:** Engage in a conversation where your sole focus is on actively listening without interrupting or preparing your response.

4. **Expressing Empathy**: Choose someone in your life who could benefit from your empathy. Engage in a conversation where you actively express understanding and empathy.

5. **Conflict Resolution Exercise**: Imagine a scenario involving conflict. Reflect on how you could use social awareness and empathy to navigate and resolve the conflict.

QUESTIONS

1. How does social awareness contribute to fostering healthier and more meaningful relationships?

2. What nonverbal cues have you noticed in your recent interactions, and how did they enhance your understanding of the conversation?

3. How does practicing empathetic listening create a deeper level of connection with others?

4. In what ways can active engagement positively impact your communication and relationships?

5. How might applying social awareness during conflicts lead to more constructive resolutions?

ACTION PLANS

1. Dedicate time to observe nonverbal cues in different social contexts to enhance your ability to read emotions.

2. Make empathetic reflection a habit after conversations to deepen your understanding of others' emotions.

3. Incorporate active listening into your interactions to create an atmosphere of authenticity and understanding.

4. Practice expressing empathy in conversations, particularly with those who might need emotional support.

5. Create a strategy for using social awareness and

empathy to navigate conflicts more effectively.

AFFIRMATIONS

1. "I connect with others on a deeper level through the power of social awareness."

2. "I am attuned to the unspoken emotions conveyed through nonverbal cues."

3. "My empathetic listening skills strengthen my relationships and foster trust."

4. "I engage actively in conversations, creating meaningful connections."

5. "By applying social awareness, I enhance my communication and nurture lasting relationships."

WEEK 4

EXCELLING IN RELATIONSHIP MANAGEMENT

Welcome to the final week of your journey towards mastering emotional intelligence through the art of relationship management. This week holds the key to transforming your interactions, whether in your personal or professional life, into opportunities for growth, collaboration, and positive impact. As you dive into the activities of this week, you're stepping into a realm where conflicts are resolved constructively, communication flows seamlessly, toxic influences are recognized and addressed, and your role as a supportive and influential leader comes to life.

Imagine being able to navigate through conflicts with grace and finesse, turning disagreements into opportunities for mutual understanding. Envision building connections that foster trust and collaboration, while skillfully recognizing and managing toxic influences. As you engage with the contents of this week, you'll realize that relationship management is not just about getting along; it's about creating a web of positive interactions that can shape the course of your life.

Understanding the Basics of Relationship Management

Relationships are the fabric of our lives, and managing them effectively is a cornerstone of emotional intelligence. In this section, you'll explore the fundamental principles of relationship management. By understanding the key components of healthy interactions, you'll be better equipped to nurture and strengthen your connections.

Effectively Resolving Conflicts and Disagreements

Conflicts are inevitable in any relationship, but how you handle them can make all the difference. This week, you'll delve into conflict resolution techniques that prioritize understanding and collaboration. By honing your ability to address conflicts constructively, you'll create an environment where differences are opportunities for growth rather than sources of tension.

Establishing Clear and Open Communication Channels

Clear communication is the backbone of any successful relationship. In this segment, you'll explore how to establish open lines of communication that foster transparency and trust. By enhancing your communication skills, you'll bridge gaps, prevent misunderstandings, and create an atmosphere of genuine connection.

Recognizing and Dealing with Toxic People

Toxic influences can derail even the healthiest relationships. In this part of the week, you'll learn to recognize the signs of toxic behavior and understand how it impacts your emotional well-being. By applying the tools provided, you'll be empowered to set boundaries and protect yourself from negativity.

Becoming a Supportive and Influential Leader through Relationship Management

Whether in your personal or professional life, your role as a leader is shaped by your ability to manage relationships. In this final section, you'll learn how to leverage your relationship management skills to become a supportive and influential leader. By fostering positive interactions, you'll inspire others, navigate challenges with finesse, and create a lasting impact.

As you conclude Week 4, take a moment to reflect on the journey you've embarked upon. You've explored the basics of relationship management, acquired conflict resolution techniques, established clear communication channels, learned to recognize toxic influences, and discovered how to become a supportive and influential leader. These skills are now part of your toolkit, allowing you to navigate relationships with heightened emotional intelligence.

EXERCISES

1. **Conflict Reflection**: Recall a recent conflict and reflect on how it was resolved. Consider alternative approaches that could have led to a more constructive outcome.

2. **Effective Communication Practice**: Engage in a conversation where your focus is on practicing clear

and open communication. Pay attention to your choice of words, tone, and active listening.

3. **Toxic Behavior Inventory**: Reflect on individuals in your life who might exhibit toxic behavior. Evaluate how their behavior impacts you and consider strategies for managing these dynamics.

4. **Positive Leadership Visualization**: Close your eyes and visualize yourself as a supportive and influential

leader in various scenarios. Feel the positive impact you create through your relationship management skills.

5. **Conflict Transformation Plan**: Develop a plan for transforming conflicts into opportunities for growth. Outline steps you can take to address conflicts constructively in the future.

QUESTIONS

1. How does relationship management contribute to fostering a positive and harmonious environment in both personal and professional settings?

2. What insights have you gained about effective conflict resolution techniques, and how might they improve your interactions?

3. In what ways can clear and open communication positively influence the

dynamics of your relationships?

4. How can recognizing toxic influences empower you to set boundaries and protect your emotional well-being?

5. How do relationship management skills contribute to your role as a supportive and influential leader?

ACTION PLANS

1. Commit to practicing conflict resolution techniques in your

interactions, aiming for mutually beneficial outcomes.

2. Incorporate active communication practices into your daily conversations to enhance clarity and understanding.

3. Identify strategies for recognizing and managing toxic influences in your life, and implement them proactively.

4. Apply your relationship management skills to your leadership role, inspiring

others and fostering positive interactions.

5. Develop a conflict transformation plan that you can refer to in moments of conflict to guide your approach.

AFFIRMATIONS

1. "I manage relationships with wisdom, fostering positive interactions that uplift and inspire."

2. "Conflict resolution is an opportunity for growth, and I

approach it with empathy and understanding."

3. "My communication is clear, open, and fosters connections built on trust."

4. "I recognize toxic influences and confidently set boundaries that protect my well-being."

5. "Through relationship management, I lead with influence, making a positive impact on those around me."

CONCLUSION

Congratulations on completing the four-week journey of "Emotional Intelligence Habits." You've immersed yourself in a comprehensive exploration of emotional intelligence, equipping yourself with practical tools to elevate your self-awareness, self-management, social awareness, and relationship management skills. The transformative insights and exercises contained within these pages have laid the foundation for a more emotionally intelligent and fulfilling life.

In Week 1, you embarked on the quest of self-awareness, understanding the importance of recognizing emotional triggers and cultivating mindfulness. By embracing these foundational principles, you've set the stage for deeper self-understanding, leading to more thoughtful decision-making and authentic personal growth.

Week 2 saw you mastering self-management techniques, discovering the art of emotional regulation, stress management, and self-control. As you practiced these strategies, you've gained the ability to navigate challenges with grace, respond intentionally to stressors, and establish healthy daily routines that support your emotional well-being.

The exploration of social awareness and empathy during Week 3 expanded your emotional horizons. You've learned to read nonverbal cues, practiced empathetic listening, and cultivated the skills to build stronger connections. These newfound abilities have enriched your interactions, allowing you to foster trust, understanding, and meaningful connections with those around you.

Finally, in Week 4, you ventured into the realm of relationship management. Armed with conflict resolution techniques, clear communication strategies, and the ability to recognize and address toxic influences, you've positioned yourself as a leader capable of creating positive impacts in both personal and professional spheres.

Throughout this journey, you've been challenged to reflect, practice, and implement what you've learned. Your commitment to growth and self-improvement is commendable, and the transformation you've undergone is a testament to your dedication.

As you move forward, remember that emotional intelligence is a continuous journey. The insights and skills you've acquired within these four weeks are seeds that, with consistent care and practice, will continue to flourish. Every interaction, every decision, and every moment of self-awareness is an opportunity to refine and deepen your emotional intelligence.

Thank you for embarking on this enriching journey of self-discovery and growth with "Emotional Intelligence Habits." May the wisdom you've gained serve as a guiding light, illuminating your path to a more emotionally intelligent, fulfilling, and empowered life.

NOTES

_____

___

_____

___

_____

__

_____

__

_____

__

_____

__

_____

__

_____

__

_____

__

_____

——

_____

——

_____

——

_____

——

_____

——

_____

——

_____

——

_____

___

_____

___

_____

___

_____

___

_____

___

_____

___

_____

___

_____

___

_____

___

_____

___

_____

___

_____

___

_____

___

_____

___

_____

____

_____

____

_____

____

_____

____

_____

____

_____

____

_____

____

_____

___

_____

___

_____

___

_____

___

_____

___

_____

___

_____

___

_____

___

_____

___

_____

___

_____

___

_____

___

_____

___

_____

___

116

119

_____

___

_____

___

_____

___

_____

___

_____

___

_____

___

_____

___

_____

___

_____

___

_____

___

_____

___

_____

___

_____

___

_____

___

_____

___

_____

__

_____

__

_____

__

_____

__

_____

__

_____

__

_____

__

_____

___

_____

___

_____

___

_____

___

_____

___

_____

___

_____

___

131

_____

__

_____

__

_____

__

_____

__

_____

__

_____

__

_____

__

_____

___

_____

___

_____

___

_____

___

_____

___

_____

___

_____

___

133

_____

___

_____

___

_____

___

_____

___

_____

___

_____

___

_____

___

139

Made in the USA
Middletown, DE
23 October 2023

41321266R00080